Dear Parent:

Congratulations! Your child is taking the first steps on an exciting journey. The destination? Independent reading!

STEP INTO READING® will help your child get there. The program offers books at five levels that accompany children from their first attempts at reading to reading success. Each step includes fun stories, fiction and nonfiction, and colorful art. There are also Step into Reading Sticker Books, Step into Reading Math Readers, and Step into Reading Phonics Readers—a complete literacy program with something to interest every child.

Learning to Read, Step by Step!

Ready to Read Preschool–Kindergarten
• big type and easy words • rhyme and rhythm • picture clues
For children who know the alphabet and are eager to begin reading.

Reading with Help Preschool–Grade 1
• basic vocabulary • short sentences • simple stories
For children who recognize familiar words and sound out new words with help.

Reading on Your Own Grades 1–3
• engaging characters • easy-to-follow plots • popular topics
For children who are ready to read on their own.

Reading Paragraphs Grades 2–3
• challenging vocabulary • short paragraphs • exciting stories
For newly independent readers who read simple sentences with confidence.

Ready for Chapters Grades 2–4
• chapters • longer paragraphs • full-color art
For children who want to take the plunge into chapter books but still like colorful pictures.

STEP INTO READING® is designed to give every child a successful reading experience. The grade levels are only guides. Children can progress through the steps at their own speed, developing confidence in their reading, no matter what their grade.

Remember, a lifetime love of reading starts with a single step!

*To my great-nephew, Justin, who is
a really "cool cat"!
—M.B.*

*Special thanks to Donald Lindburg, Ph.D.,
Associate Director of Conservation and Science,
Zoological Society of San Diego.
Thanks also to my terrific editor, Jennifer Dussling.*

*For Sue, Steven, and Julie
and all at Wildlife Art Ltd.
—M.L.R.*

Text copyright © 2002 by Mary Batten. Illustrations copyright © 2002 by Michael Langham Rowe. All rights reserved under International and Pan-American Copyright Conventions. Published in the United States by Random House Children's Books, a division of Random House, Inc., New York, and simultaneously in Canada by Random House of Canada Limited, Toronto. Originally published by Golden Books, an imprint of Random House Children's Books, a division of Random House, Inc., New York, in 2002.

www.stepintoreading.com

Educators and librarians, for a variety of teaching tools, visit us at
www.randomhouse.com/teachers

Library of Congress Cataloging-in-Publication Data
Batten, Mary.
Wild cats / by Mary Batten ; illustrated by Michael Langham Rowe.
    p.   cm. — (Step into reading. A step 4 book)
SUMMARY: Introduces the world's big cats, including lions, tigers, cheetahs, leopards, jaguars, and some more unusual varieties.
ISBN 0-375-82551-7 (trade) — ISBN 0-375-92551-1 (lib. bdg.)
1. Felidae—Juvenile literature.   [1. Cat family (Mammals).]   I. Rowe, Michael Langham, ill.
II. Title.   III. Series: Step into reading. Step 4 book.
QL737.C23 B32 2004   599.75—dc21   2002153786

Printed in the United States of America   11 10 9 8 7 6 5 4 3 2
First Random House Edition

Wild Cats

by Mary Batten

illustrated by Michael Langham Rowe

Random House New York

1
Cool Cats

They slink. They stalk. They pounce.
They growl. They hiss. They purr. They
are cats, and they are everywhere—
from snow-covered mountains to
tropical rainforests, from scorching
deserts to dry grasslands.

There are many different kinds of
wild cats, but all of them are hunters.

All are meat-eaters. They have large eyes
that can see in dim light or darkness. They
have better hearing than people. They
walk on their toes, moving silently like
furry dancers on soft, padded feet. And

all cats have sharp, dagger-like teeth
that bite and tear their prey.

Wild cats come in many sizes.
The smallest ones—the rusty-spotted
cats—weigh less than three pounds.

They are only half as big as a pet cat. The largest—tigers—weigh up to seven hundred pounds. Tigers can grow to be ten to eleven feet long. And that's not including their three-foot-long tails!

Even the biggest cat can play like a little kitten. But when it hunts, a wild cat is terrifying. Brain, muscles, and nerves work together with one purpose—to bring down an animal so that the cat can eat and survive.

And that is what makes these cats wild cats.

2
Family Cats

If you ever hear a lion roar, you'll never forget it. A lion's roar can be heard more than three miles away. It is one of the scariest sounds in nature. Zebras, gazelles, and other animals that lions hunt take cover or run for their lives.

But to another lion, the roar sends a message. The roar says, "I am here."

From far away, other lions roar back. This is how lions talk to each other.

Lions are social cats. Most other cats live alone, but lions live in groups called prides. A pride may have as few as three or as many as thirty lions. Lions spend most of the day sleeping. They don't have to worry about other animals attacking them. Who would bother a sleeping lion?

Female lions do most of the hunting for the pride. Sometimes they hunt as a team. They creep up on their prey. They wait for just the right moment to spring. When they pounce, they seize the victim with their paws and bite its side, shoulder, or neck. Although an antelope can run fast, it stands little chance against a group of female lions.

Lions are fierce hunters, but they like to cuddle, too. When two lions from the same pride meet, they rub their foreheads together and lick each other. Resting lions may drape a paw over each other's shoulders or lie back to back.

Cubs rub the top of their head against a grown lion's chin. If a lion doesn't want to be rubbed, it bares its teeth or growls. This means, "Stay away. I'm not in the mood."

Unlike most wild cats, female lions help to take care of each other's cubs. A mother lion will nurse any lion cub in the pride. When the cubs are five or six weeks old, the lionesses bring them together in a nursery group.

Older females, called aunties, act
as baby-sitters. They watch the cubs
while the younger lionesses hunt.

A female cub stays in the pride
where she was born for her whole life.
But when a male cub is between two
and four years old, he leaves the pride.
Male cubs that are born together may
stay together until they die. Sometimes
they form a group with males from
other prides. These male groups
compete to take over a pride of
females.

Only male lions have manes.
A mane shows a lion's rank in the pride.

Other males are careful around a lion with a long mane. As a lion gets older, his mane gets darker. Female lions seem to prefer lions with darker manes. When a male lion is *very* old, his mane may fade. It may even fall out.

Most lions live in Africa. Many live in protected parks. Of all wild cats, they are in the least danger. Lions are here to stay.

3
Stripes

Imagine a cat that can eat forty pounds of meat in one sitting. That would be like eating two hundred hamburgers at a time! Tigers are the largest cats— bigger even than lions. And they have the biggest appetites!

A tiger's sharp canine teeth are about three inches long. They are lethal weapons.

After a big meal, a tiger usually won't eat again for several days. But when it does, it will eat just about anything— cattle, deer, pigs, frogs, or fish.

Tigers are loners. Each tiger has its own territory. This territory is the only place a tiger can hunt without other tigers around. A tiger needs a lot of space to find food. Its territory can be as small as 20 square miles or as big as 1,500 square miles.

A tiger marks its territory so that other tigers know to stay out. It makes scratch marks on tree trunks and sprays trees and bushes with its scent.

Tigers live in hot, wet rainforests, like the ones on islands in Indonesia. They also live in cold forests in Russia and China. Unlike many cats, tigers like water. They are good swimmers.

Watch your back if you're ever in tiger territory. Tigers usually attack from behind. In India and Bangladesh, tigers sometimes kill people who go into the swamps. To help protect people in this area, the government gives out masks. They tell people to wear the masks on the *back* of their head. Why? Tigers are less likely to attack if they see a face.

With the masks, the number of people killed each year by tigers has dropped from about forty-five per year to between three and seven.

Tigers are the only wild cats with stripes. The stripes are like human fingerprints—no two tigers have exactly the same pattern. But not all tigers are orange and black. A few are white.

White tigers are not a separate kind of tiger. They are just tigers that carry the gene for white fur. Scientists think that all the white tigers in zoos today can be traced back to one white male tiger named Mohan.

Mohan was found in 1951 by an Indian prince. The prince wanted more of these unusual tigers, so he bred Mohan to one of Mohan's own

orange-and-black daughters. Four
white cubs were born. This meant both
Mohan and his daughter carried the
gene for white fur.

White tigers are very rare. In the past one hundred years, only a dozen or so have been seen in the wild. Only one in every ten thousand cubs is a white tiger.

4
Fast Cats

Watch out! These cats can move! Cheetahs are the quickest mammals on land. They can sprint as fast as seventy miles per hour. Compared to other large cats, cheetahs are small and fragile, but they are built for the chase. Their speed helps them catch and kill other animals.

Most cats have claws that can be pulled back into their paws. A cheetah does not. Why? The bit of the claws that sticks out helps the cheetah hold on to the ground when it speeds up or makes a quick turn.

In one stride, a cheetah covers almost twenty-five feet. Its paws barely touch the ground. For a second, the cat glides on air.

Cheetahs work hard to catch a meal. They can outrun most other animals.

But they can't keep up their speed for very long. They have to catch their prey quickly and bring it down. They may go through ten or more chases before they have a good meal.

Cheetahs don't roar like lions and tigers. Instead, they make little chirping, birdlike sounds. They also purr loudly. And when a cheetah is annoyed, it hisses and spits just like a house cat.

Many cheetahs live in protected parks. But they share some of these parks with lions and hyenas. And lions and hyenas sometimes kill cheetah cubs. Only one out of every twenty cheetah cubs born in the wild survives to adulthood.

A cheetah mother cares for her cubs very much the way a house cat cares for her kittens. She keeps the cubs clean by grooming, or licking, their fur.

Like kittens, the cubs are playful. The mother is patient. She lets them climb over her and bite her ears and tail.

Cheetahs may have some things in common with house cats, but no pet cat can run like that!

5
Spots

Can you guess which cat can swim, climb trees, and live in more different types of places than any other kind of large cat? If you thought of a leopard, you're right. Of all the wild cats, the leopard is the only one that lives in both rainforests and deserts.

Leopards are the largest cats that climb trees. They ambush their prey by leaping down from branches. The clouded leopard can even hang upside down from branches by its hind feet! Leopards store food in trees, too. Some African leopards have been seen hauling young giraffes up a tree.

Leopards have spotted or blotched fur. Spots break up their body shape and help them blend into patches of light and shadow in the forest.

The color of a leopard's fur depends on where it lives. Snow leopards have long, woolly, light-colored fur to match the snowy background of the mountains.

To help keep warm, a snow leopard sometimes wraps its tail around itself like a blanket.

Dark leopards called black panthers live in tropical rainforests. The light in a rainforest is dim because the thick, leafy treetops block the sun. A black

leopard's coloring helps it hide in the shadows. Even though a black leopard looks all black, it actually does have spots. But the spots are so dark you can hardly see them.

Not all black panthers are leopards. Some are jaguars. Jaguars are large spotted cats, like leopards. They are the largest wild cat in the Americas. Most live in the Amazon rainforest in South America.

Although jaguars look like leopards, there is a difference. Jaguars have small shapes within their spots, and they have a shorter tail.

Yaguara is the South American Indian word for jaguar. It means "beast that kills its prey in a single bound." A jaguar kills an animal by piercing its skull with sharp teeth.

Some rainforest Indians believe the jaguar's roar is the sound of thunder. Others believe the jaguar is the god of darkness and its spots represent the stars in the heavens. Most rainforest Indians teach their children to fear and respect the jaguar.

6
Odd Cats

Imagine a cat with a flat head! Or a cat with hair on the soles of its feet! These and other weird cats really exist. They are not as big or as famous as lions and tigers, but they're just as wild.

The puma has many names—cougar, mountain lion, and panther. It can't roar, but it makes a sound like a woman's scream. The Florida panther is actually a puma. Florida was one of the first states to pass a law to protect pumas.

A serval is a kind of short-tailed cat that lives in Africa. It has very large ears. They help it hear the soft sounds of rodents moving through the grass.

The serval leaps high in the air as it pounces on its victim. It also grabs bugs out of the air by clapping its front paws together.

It's not hard to guess where a sand cat lives—the desert! Its pale fur blends into its surroundings. A thick layer of black hair covers the soles of its feet. The cat's footpads help it walk on sand without sinking. They also protect its paws against heat or cold. In summer, the sand may be a roasting 180 degrees Fahrenheit, but at night, the desert temperature can drop below freezing.

Although gerbils make up most of its diet, the sand cat is known for killing snakes, particularly horned vipers. The sand cat doesn't drink water. It gets the moisture it needs from its prey.

The sand cat is a great digger. It builds underground burrows, where it stays during the day. At night, the sand cat comes out to hunt. Its large ears help it hear the faint sounds of rodents underground.

Looking at an African wildcat, you might mistake it for a pet. That's no surprise. Scientists think these little wild cats may be the ancestor of house cats. Like house cats, they feast on mice, but they also eat bugs, spiders, birds, snakes, lizards, and frogs.

One of the most unusual cats is the flat-headed cat. It has a flat skull and sloping snout. This cat has webbed toes that help it to swim in the swampy areas of tropical Asia where it lives. About the size of a large pet cat, it puts its entire head underwater when it hunts for fish or shrimp.

A cat with webbed feet and a flat head? Now that's one really odd cat!

7
Wild Cats in the Wild?

People have always been crazy for cats.
Some even believed cats had special
powers. In ancient Egypt, cats were
worshiped as gods. And more than
six hundred years ago, Aztec warriors
in Mexico dressed in jaguar pelts. They
believed the skins would make them
fierce and strong like the jaguar.

In modern times, killing animals to make fur coats wiped out a lot of wild cats. But then the trade in cat fur was banned by an international treaty.

Now the greatest threat to leopards, jaguars, tigers, and other wild cats is losing their homes to people. Except for lions, all the large wild cats are endangered.

Meanwhile, poachers still hunt tigers. Their fur is prized, and some people in the Far East believe tiger bones and other body parts can cure diseases. A poacher earns a whole year's wages by shooting one tiger.

In parts of the world where people
are very poor, shooting a tiger seems
like a great opportunity—even if it
is illegal.

But all over the world, people are
working to protect tigers and cheetahs

and the other large cats. Because
deep down, people love cats. We love
to see them in the wild. We love to
visit them in zoos. We even love to
share our homes with their small
cousins.

Look into a pet cat's eyes. Watch how it stalks a bird or pounces on a toy mouse. You'll see that even a pet cat can be a wild cat at heart.